The Halogen Oven

Soup

Cookbook

BY MARYANNE MADDEN

Dear Reader

Thank you for reading "**The Halogen Oven Soup Cookbook**" – it was a lot of fun creating these dishes (and eating them) and I hope you enjoy them.

If you'd like to be the first to hear when the next book is available please CLICK HERE { http://eepurl.com/MJ1TX }

My cookbooks are sometimes available for free on Kindle, so keep in touch to find out when! I promise not to send you any rubbish, but I will entertain you from time to time with stories from my kitchen.

Also check out my blog http://www.maryannemadden.com

Coming soon:

The Slow Cooker 5:2 Diet Cookbook
The Slow Cooker Low Fat Cookbook

For Andrew, Sophie, Max & Henry

Contents

INTRODUCTION

I first bought a Halogen Oven back in 2007 and at the time there were no Halogen oven cookbooks at all. So having a love of cooking and writing I decided to self publish my first book Halogen Heaven. It was an amazing success and led to a 3 book deal with the publishers Hamlyn and eventually to a number of other successful Halogen Oven cookbooks for Halogen Oven Manufacturers.

Since then I've written many more Halogen Oven recipe books (Quick & Easy & Healthy Halogen) plus quite a few for slow cookers too, so it was no surprise that I would eventually come back to writing for the Halogen Oven. I just love that little table top cooker!

This book is the latest in my Halogen Oven series, the first being **The Halogen Oven Curry Cookbook**, closely followed by **The Halogen Oven Mexican Cookbook** & **The Halogen Oven Low Fat Cookbook** all of which can be found on Amazon and kindle.

Look out for the new books, **The Halogen Oven Family Cookbook**, coming soon.

Enjoy

Maryanne

ABOUT YOUR HALOGEN OVEN

A Halogen oven is a compact table top cooker which cooks food quickly and is healthier than traditional cooking methods. It uses powerful halogen technology to produce infra-red light waves that heat up food quickly. Basically it's a glass container with a heating element built into the lid and fan that distributes heat quickly and evenly throughout the oven.

Generally the oven will come with a couple of removable cooking racks so that any fat produced simply drains away, making meat products healthier. It's abit like a George Foreman oven but you can cook joints of meat and baked potatoes at the same time etc...

General Guidance Cooking Times

All Halogen ovens will have their own variations when it comes to settings but that doesn't mean you can't use this guide.

For the sake of ease, I have based these instructions on my own oven which has settings of HI/ MEDIUM/ LOW. This equates to HI being approx 400F. If you are at all unsure about which setting to use, by all means follow my instructions, but refer to your own user manual too, and I would suggest cooking for the least amount of time recommended and then checking whether the food is done.

Equipment needed

Obviously your oven will come with various pieces of equipment, but I would expect you to have the basic oven and then two grilling shelves. If you do not have these contact your manufacturer or the company you bought the oven from to purchase them. They make cooking vegetables and meat much easier.

I use the same equipment that I use with a normal oven and haven't had to buy anything special.

Helpful Cooking Tips

Always check how well the food is cooked at minimum time.
Clean the oven interior and lamp covers frequently (after every use if possible).

RECIPES

Spicy Mexican Bean Soup

Ingredients

1 onion
2–3 garlic cloves
1 medium carrot
1 medium sweet potato
1 red pepper
300ml stock

400g Red kidney beans
1 tsp vegetable oil
1 tsp spoon chilli powder
1 tsp spoon ground cumin
1 tsp spoon dried oregano
400g chopped tomatoes

Instructions

1. In a frying pan add a little oil and leave until it begins to steam and then peel the onion and chop into small pieces, then peel and finely chop the garlic and fry until soft.

2. Transfer to the Halogen Oven and then peel and chop the carrots and the sweet potato into 1cm chunks.

3. Wash the pepper, deseed and slice into 1cm/½in pieces.

4. Add these ingredients to the Halogen Oven.

5. Next pour 300ml of stock into the Halogen Oven, together with the chilli, cumin and oregano.

6. Stir in the chopped tomatoes, and then cook for 45 minutes or until the vegetables are soft.

7. Remove from the Halogen Oven and blend the soup until smooth.

8. Return to Halogen Oven and add the drained and rinsed kidney beans.

9. Cook to warm through for 5 minutes.

Pumpkin Soup

Ingredients

3kg pumpkin (flesh roughly chopped)
125g butter
2 medium onions, peeled, finely chopped
1 cinnamon stick

freshly grated nutmeg
salt and freshly ground black pepper
1 litres Chicken/Veg stock
2 tablespoons sherry

Instructions

1. Cut the pumpkin flesh roughly (2cm)

2. Melt the butter in the base of the Halogen Oven (on high for 5 minutes) and then add the onions.

3. Next add the pumpkin flesh, the cinnamon and nutmeg, and sherry.

4. Add the stock and cook for 1 hour or until the pumpkin is cooked through.

5. Blend until smooth and then serve immediately.

Parsley & Pea Soup

Ingredients

50g butter
1 shallot, chopped
2-3 garlic cloves, finely chopped
500g flat leaf parsley, roughly chopped

400g frozen peas
1 litre hot vegetable stock
50ml double cream
25ml olive oil

Instructions

1. In a frying pan, heat the butter and then add the shallot and garlic and fry gently until softened.

2. Transfer to the Halogen Oven and then add the parsley, peas and hot stock and cook for around 45 minutes.

3. Transfer to food processor and blend until smooth

4. To serve drizzle with cream and olive oil.

French Onion Soup

Ingredients

25g butter
2 tbsp olive oil
1kg white onions, finely sliced
2 fresh thyme sprigs, leaves picked
3 garlic cloves, finely chopped
50ml dry sherry
250ml white wine

2 tbsp plain flour
1.2 litres fresh veal or beef stock
1 tsp soft brown sugar
sea salt and freshly ground black pepper
4 slices baguette, cut thickly on the diagonal
110g Gruyère, grated

Instructions

1. In a frying pan add the butter, olive oil, onions and thyme and fry until softened and golden-brown.

2. Then add the garlic and cook for another couple of minutes.

3. Transfer to the Halogen Oven then add the sherry and white wine and cook on high until the volume of the liquid has reduced by half (about half an hour).

4. Add the flour and then pour in the stock, then stir well.

5. Cook on low for another 45 minutes.

6. For the croutons, preheat a grill to its highest setting.

7. Place the bread onto a grill tray and toast lightly until golden brown and then add the cheese and return to the grill until bubbling and golden brown.

8. Serve the soup in bowls topped with the cheesy crouton

Butternut Squash Soup

Ingredients

1 pinch salt
1 butternut squash, peeled, cut into fine chunks
2 carrots, peeled and chopped
1 shallot, chopped
2 garlic cloves, chopped
2 sprigs fresh thyme

1 bay leaf
2 sage leaves
1 litre chicken stock
freshly ground black pepper
110g English cheddar

Instructions

1. Add the chopped squash, carrot, shallot, garlic, thyme, bay leaf and sage to the Halogen Oven bowl and cook on high for 4-5 minutes.

2. Cover with the stock and cook for 1 hour, or until the vegetables have softened.

3. Season with salt and freshly ground black pepper.

4. Transfer to a food processor and blend until smooth.

5. To serve, sprinkle with the cheddar, shaved with a potato peeler.

Sausage and Lentil Soup

Ingredients

1 tbsp olive oil
8 thick pork sausages (pre-cooked)
25g/1oz butter
1 onion, finely diced
1 carrot, finely diced
2 garlic cloves, peeled and finely chopped

2 sprigs thyme
1 x 410g/14oz tin cooked lentils in water, drained and rinsed
1 litre/1¾ pints stock
salt and pepper

Instructions

1. Add the onion and carrot to the Halogen Oven and cook for 2- 3 minutes.

2. Then add the garlic and thyme sprigs.

3. Next pour in the lentils and mix well.

4. Add the stock and then add the sliced sausages and set to cook for 1 hour or until the soup has thickened slightly. (Remember to add hot water if the mixture is becoming too thick).

5. Remove the thyme sprigs, then season to taste with salt and pepper and serve hot

Winter Veg Soup

Ingredients

2 tbsp sunflower oil
1 onion, finely sliced
3 garlic cloves, finely sliced
2 carrots, cut into 1.5cm
2 turnips, cut into 1.5cm
1 large potato cut into 1.5cm
1 large parsnip, cut into 1.5cm
2 tsp paprika (sweet), plus extra to serve

1 tsp hot smoked paprika
1 x 400g tin chopped tomatoes
1 tbsp tomato purée
125g chorizo sausage cut into 5mm slices
100g Puy lentils, rinsed and drained
3 pints chicken stock
Soured cream to taste.

Instructions

1. Add the onion and garlic, the carrots, turnips, potatoes and parsnip (1.5cm chunks) to the Halogen Oven.

2. Then stir in both the sweet and smoked paprika and add the tomatoes and the tomato purée.

3. Add the chorizo, Puy lentils and the stock and mix well, then cook for 1 hour to 1.5 hours.

4. Blend if you would like a smooth soup, otherwise season the soup with salt and lots of freshly ground black pepper.

5. Serve with a tbsp of soured cream and a sprinkling of paprika.

Pea and Ham Soup

Ingredients

1 tbsp vegetable oil or butter
1 medium onion, finely chopped
1 large potato (250g), peeled, cut into small cubes
salt and freshly ground black pepper

300g frozen garden peas
400ml chicken stock
200ml semi-skimmed or whole milk
100g thick cut, good quality ham

Instructions

1. Set the Halogen Oven to low and then add the butter, onion and potato, season with salt and pepper, then stir to coat the vegetables in the oil.

2. Add the peas and stock and then cook on low for 1 hour.

3. Transfer to a blender and blend until very smooth.

4. Pour back into the Halogen Oven bowl and then add the milk and tear in most of the ham.

5. Bring the soup back to a simmer for 5 minutes.

6. To serve, scatter with the rest of the ham.

Cauliflower Soup

Ingredients

1 onion, finely chopped
2 tbsp balsamic vinegar
1 garlic clove, finely chopped
800g cauliflower florets, roughly chopped

1 litre vegetable stock
250ml double cream
2 tbsp extra virgin olive oil

Instructions

1. Add the onion and garlic to the Halogen Oven.

2. Next add the cauliflower and vegetable stock and cook for 1 hour or until the cauliflower is tender.

3. Transfer to a food processor and then blend until a puree is formed.

4. Add 200ml of the cream and then season with salt and freshly ground black pepper.

5. Return to the Halogen Oven and cook on medium for 10 minutes and then serve drizzled with the balsamic vinegar, the remaining double cream and a little olive oil.

Roast Red Pepper

Ingredients

4 red peppers, core and seeds removed, roughly chopped
4 shallot, sliced
2 tsp fresh thyme leaves

1 tbsp olive oil
salt and freshly ground black pepper
200ml hot chicken stock
100ml double cream

Instructions

1. Add the chopped peppers and shallots to the Halogen Oven

2. Then add the stock and mix well, and then cook on low for around 30 minutes.

3. Next add the double cream, season well with salt and freshly ground black pepper.

4. Transfer to a food processor and then blend until smooth.

5. Serve with chunky bread or flatbreads.

Asparagus Soup

Ingredients

500g white asparagus
50g unsalted butter
1 shallot, finely chopped
700ml chicken stock
70ml crème fraîche

2 egg yolks
2 tbsp chopped parsley, to garnish
sea salt flakes
white pepper

Instructions

1. Peel each asparagus stalk from the tip to the cut end.

2. Chop off the tips and then set them aside, then cut the stalks into 1cm pieces.

3. Melt the butter in the Halogen Oven and add the shallots.

4. Next add the chopped asparagus stalks, and then pour in the stock and cook for 45 minutes on low, until the stalks are very tender.

5. Transfer to a food processor and blend until very smooth.

6. Return to the Halogen Oven and then add the reserved asparagus tips.

7. Cook gently for about 15 minutes on low or until the asparagus tips are just cooked through.

8. Mix the crème fraîche and egg yolks in a small bowl.

9. Stir this mixture into the soup and continue to stir gently for a couple of minutes until the egg yolks have thickened the soup.

10. Serve the soup garnished with a sprinkling of parsley.

Chorizo Soup

Ingredients

3-4 tbsp sunflower oil
2 medium onions, chopped
1 carrot, chopped
1 small floury potato, peeled and diced
5 sticks celery, thinly sliced
250g chorizo, roughly chopped

400g cooked, peeled chestnuts
2 tsp ground cumin
1 tsp smoked paprika
1 garlic clove, crushed
2 pints chicken or turkey stock
salt and freshly ground black pepper

Instructions

1. In the Halogen Oven add the onions, carrot, potato and celery and mix well.

2. Next add the chorizo, chestnuts, cumin, paprika and garlic.

3. Pour in the stock and cook for 1 hour until the vegetables are tender.

4. Next transfer to a food processor and blend until smooth.

5. Season, to taste, with salt and freshly ground black pepper.

Potato Soup

Ingredients

25g butter
5 rashers fatty, smoked streaky bacon
1 large onion, chopped
500g floury potatoes, peeled, cut into small
pieces

1litre light chicken stock
salt and freshly ground white pepper
1 bay leaf
4-5 tbsp soured cream
1-2 tbsp snipped fresh chives

Instructions

1. In the Halogen Oven add the butter and leave to melt and then add the bacon & onion.

2. Peel the potatoes and chop into small pieces.

3. Rinse the potatoes under cold running water until the water runs clear and then drain.

4. Add to the halogen Oven and then pour in the stock and add salt and freshly ground pepper and the bay leaf.

5. Set to low and then cook for 1 hour or until the potatoes begin to break up.

6. Remove the bay leaf and then blend half of the mixture.

7. Return to Halogen Oven and mix well.

8. Serve with a spoonful of soured cream and sprinkle with chives.

Sweet Potato and Leek Soup

Ingredients

2 handfuls of spinach
290ml chicken stock
½ sweet potato, cubed

3 leeks, sliced
15ml double cream
Parsley to serve

Instructions

1. Pour the stock into the Halogen Oven.

2. Add the sweet potato and leeks and cook for 1 hour.

3. Transfer to a food processor and then blend until smooth and then stir in the double cream.

4. Sprinkle over parsley to serve.

Leek and Potato Soup

Ingredients

700ml pints of stock chicken
25g butter
1 tbsp olive oil
1 small onion, finely chopped
4 large leeks, finely sliced

2 large potatoes, peeled and cut into cubes
1 bouquet garni
8 small rock oysters
250ml fish stock
chopped chives, to garnish

Instructions

1. Set the Halogen Oven to high and then melt the butter with the olive oil and then add the onion.

2. After a couple of minutes add the leeks, potatoes and bouquet garni and then pour in the hot stock.

3. Cook for around an hour and then remove the bouquet garni, and then blend until smooth.

4. To serve sprinkle with chives.

Celery Soup

Ingredients

1 tbsp olive oil
1 garlic clove, chopped
1 red onion, chopped

300g celery, chopped
400ml hot chicken stock
2 slices toasted ciabatta, to serve

Instructions

1. In the Halogen Oven add the garlic, onion and celery.

2. Then add the chicken stock and cook for 45 minutes.

3. Transfer to a food processor and blend until very smooth.

4. Serve with toasted ciabatta.

Broccoli Soup

Ingredients

200g broccoli florets
250ml chicken or vegetable stock
1 garlic clove, peeled and chopped

salt and freshly ground black pepper
50ml single cream

Instructions

1. In the Halogen Oven add the garlic and chicken or vegetable stock

2. Next add the broccoli florets and cook for 30 minutes or until the broccoli is tender.

3. Season to taste, and then transfer half to a blender and blend until smooth.

4. Return to the Halogen Oven and mix well, then heat through on medium for 5 minutes.

5. Drizzle with cream to serve.

Paprika & Tomato Soup

Ingredients

2 tbsp olive oil
10 rashers smoked streaky bacon, roughly chopped
5 red onions, roughly chopped
15 medium tomatoes

2 tsp smoked paprika
3 star anise
salt and freshly ground black pepper
1 x 400g can pinto beans

Instructions

1. In a frying pan heat the olive oil for a minute or so and then fry the bacon and onions until coloured.

2. Roughly chop the tomatoes and add them when the bacon is starting to crisp.

3. Transfer to the Halogen Oven and add the smoked paprika and star anise, and pour in 1 litre of water and set to cook for 1 hour.

4. Tip in the drained pinto beans and cook for a further 10 minutes on medium (or until cooked through).

5. Serve with crusty bread.

Mushroom Soup

Ingredients

25g butter
1 large onion, finely chopped
1 green pepper, finely chopped
1 medium leek, finely chopped
1–2 garlic cloves, crushed
300g button mushrooms, grated

2 tbsp plain flour
450ml vegetable stock
450ml milk
1 tbsp finely chopped parsley
salt and freshly ground black pepper
crusty bread, to serve

Instructions

1. In the Halogen Oven add the onion, green pepper, leek and garlic.

2. Next add the mushrooms to and stir in the flour.

3. Then add the stock a little at a time, stirring well between each addition.

4. Turn to high and leave for 15 minutes and then pour in the milk and then cook for another 30 minutes on medium.

5. Stir in the chopped parsley and season to taste with salt and freshly ground black pepper.

6. Serve with crusty bread.

Tomato and Sweetcorn Soup

Ingredients

2 cloves garlic, crushed
1 large onion, finely chopped
olive oil
1 tsp powdered cumin
2 x 400g tins chopped tomatoes

340g sweetcorn tinned
1Litre vegetable or chicken stock
2 tbsp tomato purée
fresh basil
salt and black pepper

Instructions

1. In a frying pan add 1 tbsp of olive oil and cook until it begins to steam.

2. Then add the garlic and onion and cook until soft and translucent.

3. Transfer to the Halogen Oven and then add the cumin, tomatoes, sweetcorn, stock and tomato purée.

4. Cook for 1.5 hours on low.

5. Remove half the soup and set to one side and blend the other half until smooth.

6. Return all the soup to the Halogen Oven and mix well.

7. Scatter with fresh basil.

Fennel Soup

Ingredients

1 tbsp butter
½ shallot, finely chopped
100g new potatoes, peeled and chopped
½ large fennel bulb, chopped

150ml hot chicken stock
salt and freshly ground black pepper
small handful fresh dill, chopped

Instructions

1. In a frying pan heat the butter for 60-90 seconds and then gently cook the shallot until softened.

2. Add the chopped new potatoes and fennel and mix and then cook for 2-3 minutes.

3. Transfer to the Halogen Oven and add the stock and cook for 1 hour, or until the vegetables are tender.

4. Season, to taste, with salt and freshly ground black pepper.

5. Add the dill and then blend until smooth and return to the Halogen Oven to reheat slightly.

Sweet Potato and Coconut Soup

Ingredients

1 tbsp oil
1 onion, peeled and finely chopped
1 garlic clove, crushed
1.25cm piece fresh ginger, peeled
675g sweet potatoes, peeled and diced

1 tbsp lemongrass, chopped
570ml vegetable stock
570ml coconut cream
salt and freshly ground black pepper
2 limes, zest and juice

Preparation method

1. In a frying pan heat the oil for 1 minute and then gently sauté the onion, garlic and ginger for around 5 minutes until tender.

2. Transfer to Halogen Oven on low and then add the sweet potatoes and lemongrass and the stock and cook for 1 hour or until the vegetables are tender.

3. Transfer to a food processor and blend with half of the coconut cream until smooth.

4. Return to the Halogen Oven and add the remaining coconut cream and then season with salt and pepper.

5. Finally add the lime juice and garnish with the lime zest.

Watercress Soup

Ingredients

20g unsalted butter
100g white onion, finely chopped
1 garlic clove, finely chopped
300g watercress, tough stalks removed
sea salt and freshly ground black pepper

100g spinach leaves
500ml boiling water
500g ice cubes
100ml crème fraîche

Instructions

1. In the Halogen Oven add the chopped onion and garlic.

2. Next add the watercress and a pinch of salt and then add the spinach.

3. Next pour in the boiling water and cook for 15 minutes on high.

4. Transfer to a food processor and then add the ice.

5. Blend until smooth and then return to the Halogen Oven and heat for 10 minutes.

6. Serve with the crème fraîche swirled through.

Curried Carrot Soup

Ingredients

150g unsalted butter
150g onions, chopped
2 garlic cloves, crushed
500g carrots, peeled and chopped into small pieces

1 tsp toasted cumin seeds
½ tsp Madras curry powder
300ml chicken stock
1 bouquet garni
1 tbsp chopped fresh coriander

Instructions

1. In a frying pan melt the butter for 60-90 seconds and then cook the onion, garlic and carrots, with a pinch of salt, for 5-6 minutes, or until softened.

2. Add the toasted cumin seeds and Madras curry powder, stock, bouquet garni and fry until fragrant.

3. Transfer to the Halogen Oven and add 500ml of water and cook for 1 hour.

4. Remove the bouquet garni, and transfer to a food processor and then blend the soup until really smooth.

5. Season to taste.

6. To serve sprinkle with chopped fresh coriander.

Spicy Fish Soup

Ingredients

For the curry paste
2 garlic cloves
2 bunches coriander, stems (leaves for garnish)
4 small green chillies
1 tbsp palm sugar
3 shallots, finely chopped
3 limes, juice only
dash fish sauce

salt

For the soup
2 tbsp vegetable oil
1 litre fish stock
1 carrot, finely sliced
8 raw king prawns
200g smoked sea bass

Instructions

1. In a blender combine all of the curry paste ingredients into a smooth paste.

2. Transfer to the Halogen Oven and add a little oil and to the paste and mix well. Heat on high and leave for 5 minutes or until fragrant.

3. Next add the stock and carrot and cook for 1.5 hours.

4. Finally add the prawns and Seabass and cook for a further 10 minutes.

5. To serve, garnish with the coriander and chillies.

Broccoli and Tomato Soup

Ingredients

30g butter
½ onion, finely chopped
1 garlic clove, chopped
3 stems purple sprouting broccoli, chopped
2 tbsp capers, rinsed and drained

1 ripe tomato, roughly chopped
150ml hot chicken stock
2 tbsp double cream
handful fresh chives, chopped, to serve

Instructions

1. In a frying pan heat the butter and then gently cook the onion and garlic until softened but not coloured.

2. Transfer to the Halogen Oven and add the broccoli, capers, chopped tomato and stock.

3. Cook for 45 minutes on low, or until the broccoli is tender.

4. Then stir in the cream and allow to cool slightly.

5. Transfer to a food processor and blend until smooth.

6. If necessary re-heat the soup and then serve with a sprinkle of chives.

Beetroot Soup

Ingredients

3-4 medium (apple-sized) beetroot (about 500-600g) grated coarsely, or chopped into small dice
400g chopped tomatoes, halved
1 clove garlic, chopped roughly
1 medium onion, peeled and finely chopped

2 tbsp olive or sunflower oil
500ml beef stock
salt and freshly ground black pepper
125g feta cheese

Instructions

1. In the Halogen Oven add the tomatoes and garlic and drizzle over half the olive oil

2. Next add the onion, the beetroot and the stock and cook for around 30 minutes or until the beetroot is tender.

3. Stir in the tomato purée, and then transfer to a food processor.

4. Blend until completely smooth.

5. Divide between warm bowls and crumble over a little feta into each bowl.

6. Serve with crusty bread.

Swede Soup

Ingredients

1 swede, peeled and cut into cubes (and roasted for 25 minutes)
3 tbsp olive oil
salt and freshly ground black pepper
1 onion, finely chopped
2 carrots, finely sliced

2 stalks celery, finely sliced
1 clove garlic, crushed
6 stalks fresh thyme, leaves only
1.25 litres vegetable stock
142ml carton single cream
fresh thyme leaves to garnish

Instructions

1. In the Halogen Oven add the onion, carrots, celery, garlic and thyme leaves and a tbsp of oil.

2. Add the roasted swede and pour over the stock and set to low for 1 hour.

3. Transfer to food processor and blend the soup until completely smooth and season to taste.

4. Stir in most of the cream, reserving some for garnishing, and then gently re-heat if necessary.

5. Garnish with a swirl of cream, some fresh thyme leaves and freshly ground black pepper.

Broccoli and Stilton Soup

Ingredients

1 tbsp olive oil
55g Stilton
1 tbsp butter
½ large onion, chopped
1 garlic clove, chopped

170g broccoli, florets and stem, chopped
150ml hot chicken stock
salt and freshly ground black pepper
1 free-range egg yolk
3 tbsp double cream

Instructions

1. In a frying pan heat the oil and butter until they begin to give off steam.

2. Add the garlic and onion and sauté for 2-3 minutes, or until soft.

3. Transfer to the Halogen Oven and add the broccoli and the hot chicken stock.

4. Cook for 45 minutes and then transfer to a food processor.

5. Blend until completely smooth and then season with salt and freshly ground black pepper.

6. Place the egg yolk and cream into a bowl and mix.

7. Add the egg mixture into the hot soup and stir until the soup starts to thicken.

8. Crumble over the Stilton and serve hot.

Mexican Sweet Potato Soup

Ingredients

25g butter
½ sweet potato, peeled and cubed
1 lime, cut in half
1 clove garlic

½ pint chicken stock
1 tbsp honey
Crushed Nachos

Instructions

1. In the Halogen Oven add the butter, potato, lime and the garlic and cook on high for 10 minutes.

2. Mix well and then add the chicken stock and honey.

3. Cook for 1.5 hours and then remove the lime and discard.

4. Transfer to a food processor and blend the soup until smooth.

5. Serve with sprinkling of crushed nachos.

Crab and Sweetcorn Soup

Ingredients

300g tinned sweetcorn, rinsed and drained
1 tbsp vegetable oil
3 spring onions, finely chopped
2.5cm piece ginger, peeled, cut into matchsticks
200g crabmeat
50ml dry sherry

1 litre chicken stock
1 tsp cornflour mixed with a little water to form a paste
1 free-range egg, beaten
1 tsp sesame seeds

Instructions

1. Place three-quarters of the sweetcorn into the food processor and blend to a smooth purée.

2. In the Halogen Oven add a little oil, the chopped onion, the spring onion and ginger and cook for 5 minutes on high.

3. Then add the crabmeat, sherry and the stock and set to cook for 30 minutes.

4. Add the remaining sweetcorn and the cornflour paste and stir well.

5. Pass the beaten egg through a sieve held over the soup to create strings of egg in the soup.

6. Cook until the eggs have set as strands (about 15-20 minutes on medium).

7. Garnish with sesame seeds.

Tomato and Basil Soup

Ingredients

2 tbsp olive oil to serve
1 red onion, peeled and diced
6 garlic cloves, peeled and diced
150ml/5fl oz water

12 plum tomatoes quartered
800g canned plum tomatoes
salt and freshly ground black pepper
1 tbsp chopped fresh basil

Instructions

1. In the Halogen Oven add the onion and garlic and cook on high for a few minutes.

2. Then add the water and all of the tomatoes and cook 1 hour on low, or until the volume of liquid has reduced and the tomato soup has thickened.

3. Mix well and sprinkle over the chopped basil leaves.

4. To serve, drizzle over the olive oil.

Pea and Bacon Soup

Ingredients

1 tbsp olive oil
½ onion, sliced
4 bacon rashers, chopped

1 garlic clove, chopped
150g frozen peas, defrosted, plus extra to serve
150ml hot vegetable stock

Instructions

1. In a frying pan heat the oil and fry the onion until softened but not coloured.

2. Add the bacon and fry until golden-brown and then add the garlic and cook for one minute.

3. Transfer to the Halogen Oven and add the frozen peas and vegetable stock.

4. Cook for 20 minutes on high or until the peas are tender.

5. Transfer to a food processor and then blend the soup until smooth.

6. To serve, pour the soup into a bowl and top with a few extra peas

Chunky Cabbage Soup

Ingredients

500ml chicken stock
1 carrot, peeled and thickly sliced
¼ white cabbage, shredded

2 tbsp extra virgin olive oil
3 tbsp double cream
salt and freshly ground black pepper

Instructions

1. In the Halogen Oven add the stock, carrot and cabbage

2. Cook on low for 1 hour, or until the vegetables are tender.

3. Then add the olive oil and cream and mix well.

4. Season with salt and freshly ground black pepper.

5. Transfer to a food processor and blend until most of the soup is smooth, but there are still a few chunky bits.

6. Serve with chunky bread.

Carrot and Coriander Soup

Ingredients

1 onion, sliced
450g carrots, sliced
1 tsp ground coriander

1 litres vegetable stock.
250g Red lentils
large bunch fresh coriander, roughly chopped

Instructions

1. Add the onions and the carrots and 1 litre of vegetable stock to the Halogen Oven.

2. Then add the red lentils and stir in the ground coriander.

3. Cook on low for 1.5 hours then add half the fresh coriander.

4. Finally transfer to a food processor and blend until smooth and then stir in the fresh coriander and serve.

Spiced Tomato Soup

Ingredients

100g sun dried tomatoes
4 tbsp olive oil
1 onion, roughly chopped
3 garlic cloves, roughly chopped
2 long red chillies, finely sliced
1 tbsp tomato purée

2kg mixed tomatoes, roughly chopped
handful fresh coriander leaves, roughly chopped
1 litre chicken or vegetable stock
2-3 tbsp caster sugar
75ml double cream
4 tbsp crème fraîche

Instructions

1. In the Halogen Oven add the chopped onions; sun dried tomatoes, the garlic, chillies, tomato paste and tomatoes.

2. Then add ¾ of the coriander and the stock, and cook for 30 minutes.

3. Transfer to a food processor and blend to a purée.

4. Season, to taste, with salt, freshly ground black pepper and sugar.

5. Return to the Halogen Oven and then stir in the cream and heat for 5 minutes on medium.

6. Top with a spoonful of crème fraîche; drizzle with olive oil and sprinkle over the coriander.

Red Lentil Soup

Ingredients

50g unsalted butter
1½ tbsp grated fresh ginger
¼ tsp each ground allspice, ground cumin, and chilli powder
½ tsp each curry powder and ground coriander
2 onions finely chopped
1 parsnip, chopped
1 stick celery

750g carrots, sliced
50g split red lentils, rinsed
25g long-grain rice
1 litres vegetable stock
200ml tin coconut milk
2 tbsp fresh lime juice
3 tbsp chopped coriander

Instructions

1. In a frying pan melt the butter and then add the ginger, allspice, cumin, chilli powder, curry powder, and ground coriander.

2. Transfer to the Halogen Oven and mix well and then add the vegetables and stock.

3. Next stir in the lentils and rice and cook for 1 hour or until the vegetables are tender and the lentils have started to break down.

4. Transfer to a food processor and blend the soup until smooth and then add the coconut milk, lime juice, and coriander.

5. Heat through again to serve.

Chilli Spinach Soup

Ingredients

2 tbsp olive oil
½ onion, peeled, chopped
1 garlic clove, peeled, finely chopped
½ red chilli, chopped

500ml chicken stock
2 handfuls spinach leaves, washed
salt and freshly ground black pepper
2 tbsp double cream, to serve

Instructions

1. In the Halogen Oven add the onion, garlic, chilli and stock and cook for 1 hour on low.

2. Add the spinach, stir well and cook for another 10 minutes.

3. Transfer to a food processor and blend until smooth and then season, to taste, with salt and freshly ground black pepper.

4. To serve, drizzle with a little cream.

Sweet Pepper Soup

Ingredients

1 tbsp olive oil
1 onion, chopped
½ red pepper, chopped
handful pineapple, chopped
1 tbsp curry powder

1 tsp turmeric
1 chicken stock cube
400ml water
75ml double cream

Instructions

1. In a frying pan heat the oil and add the onion and pepper. Fry gently over a medium heat for three minutes, to soften.
2. Transfer to the Halogen Oven and add the curry powder and turmeric and crumble in the stock cube and add the water and the pineapple.
3. Cook for 1 hour on medium.
4. Finally add the double cream and cook on medium for 5-10 minutes to thicken the soup.
5. Pour the soup into a serving bowl and serve immediately.

Almond Soup

Ingredients

25g butter
1 clove garlic, crushed
150ml vegetable stock

50ml double cream
75g whole almonds, toasted and finely chopped

Instructions

1. In a frying pan melt the butter on a medium heat. Add the garlic and sauté until softened.

2. Transfer to the Halogen Oven and add the vegetable stock, double cream and almonds and set to cook for 30 minutes on low.

3. Transfer to a food processor and blend until smooth.

4. Season with salt and freshly ground black pepper and sprinkle with parsley.

Chunky Chicken Soup

Ingredients

55g butter
2 onions, peeled and sliced
2 sticks celery, finely chopped
2 carrots, peeled and finely diced
25g plain flour

1.2 litres chicken stock
450g cooked chicken, skinned and shredded
1 tbsp freshly chopped parsley
salt and freshly ground black pepper

Instructions

1. Heat the Halogen Oven on high and add the chopped onions, celery and carrots and stir in the flour.

2. Add the chicken stock and mix well, set to low and cook for 45 minutes.

3. Finally add the cooked chicken and cook for a further 10 minutes.

4. Season, to taste, with salt and freshly ground black pepper.

5. Transfer half of the mixture to a food processor and blend until smooth, and then return to the Halogen Oven and then stir together and heat for 5 minutes on high.

6. Stir in the parsley and serve.

Vegetable and Coriander Soup

Ingredients

1 tbsp olive oil
½ cauliflower, cut into florets
½ onion, finely chopped
1 carrot, chopped

1 garlic clove, chopped
1 tsp coriander seeds, toasted
425ml hot chicken or vegetable stock
salt and freshly ground black pepper

Instructions

1. In a frying pan heat the olive oil and then add the onion and carrot and fry for 4-5 minutes.

2. Also add the garlic and coriander seeds and fry for one minute.

3. Transfer to the Halogen Oven and add the cauliflower florets, stock and salt and freshly ground black pepper.

4. Cook for 1 hour, or until the cauliflower is tender.

5. Transfer to a food processor and blend the soup until smooth.

6. Serve with thick crusty bread.

Broad Bean Soup

Ingredients

2 tbsp olive oil
½ onion, finely chopped
1 garlic clove, chopped

300ml hot chicken stock
200g broad beans
salt and freshly ground black pepper

Instructions

1. In the Halogen Oven add the onion and garlic and leave for 5 minutes.

2. Next add the stock, broad beans and season with salt and freshly ground black pepper.

3. Cook for 45 minutes on low or until the beans are soft.

4. Transfer to a food processor and blend until smooth.

5. Garnish with the chopped chives.

Spicy Kidney Bean Soup

Ingredients

2 tbsp olive oil
½ large onion, chopped
½ red pepper, chopped
1 garlic clove, chopped
pinch cayenne pepper

pinch chilli powder
½ can red kidney beans, rinsed and drained
100ml hot vegetable stock
100ml milk
1 tbsp chopped fresh parsley, to garnish

Instructions

1. Place the onion, pepper and garlic into the Halogen Oven and then add the cayenne pepper, chilli powder and kidney beans.

2. Add the stock and milk and cook on low (mixing occasionally) for 30 minutes.

3. Finally transfer to a food processor and blend the soup until smooth.

4. To serve, pour the soup into a bowl and garnish with the parsley.

Courgette Soup

Ingredients

750ml chicken stock
60ml extra virgin olive oil
60ml single cream
1 tbsp chopped garlic

handful basil leaves, chopped
1kg green courgettes, cut into 1cm/½in slices
handful flat leaf parsley, chopped
50g freshly grated parmesan, plus extra to serve

-

Instructions

1. In a frying pan heat the oil and cook the garlic, basil, salt and courgette slowly for 10 minutes or until the courgettes are lightly browned and softened.

2. Transfer to the Halogen Oven and then pour in the stock and cook for 1 hour on low.

3. Transfer ¾ of the soup mixture to the food processor and blend until smooth

4. Return the unblended mixture to the Halogen Oven and stir in the cream, parsley and parmesan and heat for 5 minutes.

5. To serve sprinkle over more parmesan,

6. Serve with crusty bread.

Chickpea Soup

Ingredients

200g chickpeas (pre-soaked tinned)
1 glass red wine
1 tin tomatoes
a few sprigs of rosemary

4-5 cloves garlic
1 onion
olive oil

Instructions

1. Add the pre-soaked chickpeas and sprigs of rosemary with enough water to cover them to the Halogen Oven and cook on low until they are very soft (30 minutes).

2. Then add the onion, oil, garlic and a sprig of rosemary.

3. Next add the wine and tomatoes and cook on low for 45 minutes.

4. Finally remove half of the mixture and blend and then mix together..

5. Serve with a drizzle of olive oil.

Smoked Garlic Soup

Ingredients

1 large potato, peeled and diced
2 bulbs smoked garlic, separated into cloves,
peeled

150ml hot chicken stock
salt and freshly ground black pepper
1 tsp chopped fresh chives, to garnish

Instructions

1. Place the potato, garlic cloves and hot stock into the Halogen Oven and cook for 1 hour on low.

2. Season with salt and freshly ground black pepper,

3. Transfer to a food processor and blend until smooth.

4. Garnish with chives.

Creamy Pea Soup

Ingredients

½ red onion, diced
25g butter
200g peas (tinned or frozen, thawed)

300ml chicken or vegetable stock
100ml double cream
2 tbsp parsley, chopped

Instructions

1. Melt the butter in the Halogen Oven and then add the onions.

2. Next add the peas, stock and cream and cook for 45 minutes on low.

3. Transfer to a food processor and blend the soup.

4. Serve in a large bowl garnished with the chopped parsley

Curried Parsnip Soup

Ingredients

1 tbsp olive oil
½ onion, finely sliced
1 garlic clove, finely chopped
1 tsp curry powder
2 cardamom pods, crushed, shells discarded
½ parsnip, peeled, cored and chopped

½ small potato, peeled and chopped
50ml white wine
250ml hot chicken stock
salt and freshly ground black pepper
1 tsp chopped fresh chives, to garnish

Instructions

1. In a frying pan heat the oil until it begins to steam, then cook the onion and garlic until softened.

2. Add the curry powder and cardamom seeds and stir well,

3. Transfer to the Halogen Oven and then add the parsnip and potato and stock on high.

4. Next add the white wine and cook for around 1 hour on low.

5. Transfer half of the mixture to a food processor and blend until smooth.

6. Return to the Halogen Oven and mix together.

7. Season, to taste, and top with croutons or chives to serve.

Smoky Bacon and Tomato Soup

Ingredients

1 tsp olive oil
½ onion, chopped
2 garlic cloves, chopped
4 slices bacon, chopped

½ pint chicken stock
2 tomatoes, chopped
2 tbsp tomato purée

Instructions

1. In the Halogen Oven add the oil, onion and garlic and bacon for 10 minutes.

2. Pour in the chicken stock and add the tomatoes and purée. Mix together

3. Cook on low for 45 minutes and then transfer to a food processor and blend until smooth.

4. Serve with white crusty bread.

Spinach Soup

Ingredients

2 tbsp vegetable oil
½ onion, chopped
5 tbsp chopped fresh parsley
300ml chicken or vegetable stock

85g white crusty bread, torn
salt and freshly ground black pepper
200g spinach leaves, roughly chopped
1 tbsp Greek-style yoghurt, to serve

Instructions

1. In a frying pan heat the oil and fry the onion for 5-6 minutes, or until softened, then add the spinach, parsley and stock.

2. Transfer to the Halogen Oven and cook on low for 30 minutes.

3. Serve in warm bowls and garnish with a dollop of yogurt.

Yellow Pepper Soup

Ingredients

1 garlic clove, finely chopped
1 tbsp olive oil
¼ red onion, finely chopped

½ yellow pepper, chopped
150ml chicken stock
handful rocket, finely chopped

Instructions

1. In a frying pan add the onion and oil and cook until softened.

2. Then add the garlic and fry for another minute.

3. Transfer to the Halogen Oven and add the pepper and stock and cook for 45 minutes on low.

4. Finally add the rocket and simmer for a further 2-3 minutes.

5. Serve in warm bowls with a sprinkling of rocket

Sweet and Sour Cabbage Soup

Ingredients

1 small potato, peeled, chopped
250ml hot vegetable stock
½ green cabbage, shredded
1 glass white wine

½ tsp cumin seeds
white wine vinegar
1 tsp honey

Instructions

1. Place the chopped potato, vegetable stock, cabbage and white wine into the Halogen Oven and cook for 1 hour on high.
2. Then add the cumin seeds and white wine vinegar and cook for another 30 minutes.
3. To serve, pour the soup into a serving bowl and drizzle with a little honey.

Lentil and Cumin Soup

Ingredients

1 can of lentils, rinsed and drained
100ml red wine
150ml water

handful fresh parsley, chopped
1 tsp cumin seeds
100ml double cream

Instructions

1. Pour the red wine and water into the Halogen Oven and then add the lentils, parsley and cumin seeds and cook for 1 hour on low.

2. Season with sea salt and freshly ground black pepper.

3. Add the cream and turn up the heat to high until bubbling (10-15 minutes).

4. Transfer to a food processor and blend until smooth.

5. Serve with a sprinkle of chopped chives.

Apple and Pumpkin Soup

Ingredients

1 small pumpkin
3 tbsp olive oil
½ onion, peeled, chopped

400ml chicken stock
½ apple, peeled, core removed, chopped
salt and freshly ground black pepper

Instructions

1. Cut the lid off the pumpkin and hollow out the inside: remove the seeds and set aside, spoon out the flesh and cut it into small pieces.

2. Chop the onion and add the pumpkin pieces, apple and stock to the Halogen Oven and cook on low for 1 hour, or until the pumpkin is tender.

3. Season to taste, with salt and freshly ground black pepper.

4. Transfer to a food processor and blend until smooth.

5. Serve with toasted pumpkin seeds and thick toast.

THANK YOU!

Please don't forget to leave feedback & check out my other books

DISCLAIMER
IMPORTANT -- PLEASE READ

This publication is an informational product based on the authors own experience and research. It is not affiliated with any Halogen Oven manufacturer. It has not been evaluated by any medical professionals. The Author and Publisher assume no responsibility or liability whatsoever on the behalf of any purchaser or reader of these materials. The author is not a professional chef, nor does she claim to be.

As always, before attempting anything mentioned in this book, or if you are in doubt, you should use your best judgment. If you fail to do so, you are acting at your own risk. You, the buyer or reader of this book, alone assume all risk for anything you may learn from this book.

By choosing to use the information made available in this book, you agree to indemnify, defend, and hold harmless the author of this book from all claims (whether valid or invalid), suits, judgment, proceedings, losses, damages, costs and expenses, of any nature whatsoever (including reasonable fees) for which the author of this book may become liable resulting from the use or misuse of any products sold.

ABOUT THE AUTHOR

Maryanne Madden is a food writer based in Yorkshire. Her previous books Halogen Heaven; Healthy Halogen & Quick & Easy have all been on Amazons best sellers list.

Halogen Heaven
Quick & Easy Halogen Oven cooking for one
Healthy Halogen
The Halogen Oven Curry Cookbook
The Halogen Oven Mexican Cookbook
The Halogen Oven Low Fat Cookbook
The Halogen Oven Vegetarian Cookbook

All books can be found on Amazon and Kindle in paperback and eBook formats.

Coming soon...

The Halogen Oven Family Cookbook

CPSIA information can be obtained at www.ICGtesting.com
Printed in the USA
LVOW08s0336030615

440870LV00029B/1183/P